LAZARUS ON A SPUR LINE

POEMS AND ESSAYS

Also by Dewey Whetsell

FIRE AND ICE
Memoirs of an Alaska Fire Chief

For details of this book
and other ponderings of Dewey Whetsell visit
www.deweywhetsell.com

LAZARUS ON A SPUR LINE
POEMS AND ESSAYS

Dewey G. Whetsell

NORTHBOOKS
Eagle River, Alaska

Copyright © 2006 by Dewey G. Whetsell

All rights reserved. No part of this book may be reproduced in any form without permission except by a reviewer who may quote brief passages in a media review.

Photo Credits: Personal collection of the author
Sadat (p. 39) from web page–
www.ibiblio.org/sullivan/bios/Sadat-bio.html

Art Credits: Front cover art – "Why Is That Tree There?"
Jessie Quan, Seattle, WA, 2004.

Published by:

NorthBooks
17050 N. Eagle River Loop Road, # 3
Eagle River, Alaska 99577
www.northbooks.com

Printed in the United States of America

ISBN 978-0-9720604-9-3

Library of Congress Control Number: 2006907832

Table of Contents

Foreword v
Upon Hearing Sarah Vaughan Sing "Dreamsville" 1
Scenes That Strike You Silent 4
I Would Fight More Fiercely 7
Blessing Space (essay) 8
Lazarus on a Spur Line 10
Self-Improvement Books 11
To Loren Eiseley 12
Alaskan Winter Night 14
Old Cordova — Alaska in Summer (essay) 15
On the Docks 16
The Sailor and the Whore 17
To Dr. Francis Schaeffer 22
Crossing the Line — Speaking of Schaeffer (essay) 24
A Few Yards Short of a Poem 31
To Don 35
Saturday Mornings 38
Sadat 39
Hiroshima 40
Introduction to "Reflections of Pontius Pilate" (essay) 42
Reflections of Pontius Pilate 49
Introduction to "The Assassinations" 53
The Assassinations 54
Introduction to Uncle Russ 56
Uncle Russ 57
Take My Hand 58
God Bless Grandpa, Beer, and Mrs. Murphy's Chowder . . . 59
Two Years Since My Father's Death 60
Grandmother and Grandfather Cummings 62
In Memory 63
Introduction to What's-His-Name 66
To What's-His-Name, Aged 24 67
Genesis on a Book Shelf (essay) 71

Foreword

I always thought it would be fun to write a book whose foreword was more interesting than the rest of the contents. Here is the point: In the practical world, poetry is useless.

Leonardo Da Vinci was made a household name thanks to author Dan Brown. A couple of the characters in his *Angels and Demons* epitomized Leonardo's latter-year's intellectual struggles. Da Vinci sought to connect all of his studies to identify the single, smallest common denominator among them that might connect anatomy with music, or physics with art. He went in search of the very essence of the human being. Yet, the Renaissance Man himself failed, and his failure led to a deep despondency prior to his death. He had wanted all of the dimensions of Man wrapped in a tidy package….a map-able system.

What is a person? Does art peer into the soul while science exams the machine? Does it make sense that each person is two independent entities: A mechanical entity and an ethereal entity? Well, neither Dan Brown's fictional character—priest/physicist—named "Leonardo" by Brown, nor Leonardo's adopted daughter—Bio Entanglement Physicist (studying the interconnectivity of life systems)—were able to nail down the illusive and sought-after interconnectivity of art and science.

Years before Brown's books, I was reading an essay, "The Two Cultures" by C.P. Snow. The "two cultures" were "that bipolar division between the humanities and sciences." Even the father of modern science, Francis Bacon, began to fear that eventually people like Thomas Huxley would refer contemptuously to the "caterwauling of poets." While on the other hand, those who got depressed by the world of pure technics, searched poetry for a *domain of value,* realizing that the search for values would be dismissed by the technocrats as being without significance. Technocrats believe that the more they dissect life into its elements, the closer they are getting to solving the ultimate mysteries of life. The technocrats subtract "value" out of their equations because "value" cannot be quantified, in fact, its existence cannot be substantiated.

There is a certain authoritarianism found in science, or in its illusive promises of perfection. The autonomous fragments of scientific research become institutions in themselves. They are autonomous because they feel no need to mesh with other researches. They each believe that ultimately, *theirs* will contain the lowest common denominator thus revealing the secret of life. It's like a countryside spotted with a shit-load of silos, each one containing something different. Which silo do I place my faith in? Which one contains "the answer" — physics, or chemistry, or psychiatry, or eugenics?

Okay, Leonardo, pay attention. Scientists' achievements are quantitatively transmissible. All discoveries are cumulative. You can subtract man's moon landing back to a pasture in Kitty Hawk. Artistic creation, on the other hand, is unique. It is not accumulative. Each work of art is a stand-alone creation: Its own distinct world. "Man is first and foremost the self-fabricating animal....the artist plays an enormous role in this act of self-creation. It is he who touches the hidden strings of pity, who searches our hearts, who makes us sensitive to beauty, who asks questions about fate and destiny," said Lewis Mumfort.

By contrast to the artist, Snow explained, "… some minds exhibit an almost instinctive hostility toward the mere attempt to *wonder* or to ask what lies below the microscopic world. Is there something here we fear to face, except when clothed in safely-sterilized professional speech? Have we grown reluctant in this age of power to admit mystery and beauty into our thoughts, or learn where power ceases?"

Emerson described a stairway that I pictured as being in outer space. It goes upward so far that you can't see the end of it; it just disappears into a tiny dot. And it comes from a place so far back in distance or time, you can't see its beginning down below—just a dot. Right in the middle, is this guy standing on one step, with his other foot poised on the next step up, ready to keep climbing. It is like he just woke up to find himself there and had to keep climbing because there is nowhere else to go.

Where does man's stairway go? To what end? Maybe it doesn't end.

So, Leonardo, we use our powerful telescopes or magnificent microscopes to look outward or look inward to see what makes us tick so we can make us tock. We stand between the telescope and the microscope wondering where the hell we fit in. But, without the artist, without the value, who cares? Maybe just "fitting in" doesn't address the essence of the question. I'll bet it's bigger than that.

There are lots of smock-wearers out there machine-tinkering. I'm pulling for them. I try not to be too annoyed with them as they hang suspended, squinting into their blinking devices, huddled and breathless as they crunch their formulas. But, while waiting for the next startling scientific revelation to send me cartwheeling across the room, I'm gonna caterwaul some useless poems.

Upon Hearing Sarah Vaughan
Sing "Dreamsville"

Waiting for Sarah, the scene is set with sights and sounds—
a collage in my mind:
Jazz wafting from a smoky club next to an old warehouse....
scotch and overcoats....fedoras and shades on stage....
wordless conversations of nods and half smiles....
women in satin and spikes-with-straps, soft throaty laughs....
But, it ain't over when the last note drifts away.
Still pending—
in the wee, small hours.... roof tops at 3:00 a.m.
melancholy dawn behind the skyline....
expensive shoes clacking on deserted sidewalks....
fire escapes in the rain....

But back at the club that night, still waiting for Sarah—
Kerouac in cufflinks ambles in;
Dylan Thomas is sober and pensive;
Marlon Brando in tweed examines the floor;
Charlie Mingus is writing verse in the corner;
Tennessee Williams just arrives by streetcar;
Holden Caufield bores himself and grows silent;
Mickey Spillane clutches a perfumed scarf and can't talk about it;
and as always, Carl Sagan is smugly anxious to explain it all.

Before the set—
Patrons drift away from the droning Sagan
who's explaining how the organ reed is made,
how the flute is chromed,
how they slice the page the notes are printed on,
but can't explain the source from which a song is born,
nor why strangers merge upon a lilting phrase,
nor why we follow the night singer
      through the rainbow of her soul.

We soar above science in this public love affair
and cannot compute the pang of our humanity.

Soul-brown Sarah in satin rustles softly to the mic.
Brandy-amber lights are dimmed,
Kerouac is mesmerized
Mingus closes his tablet
Dylan orders a double.

We see —
The pasty-gray clerk, who wonders why
he never burned from the bones of his passion —
    the night singer draws you up to her.
Lonely lady, middle-aged forever, whose desperate
daydreams cannot block the encroaching ice —
    the night singer caresses you in your closed eyes.
The young man, fancy in his spangled vanity
who cannot see above the waist —
    the night singer offers tenderness.
Giddy hottie, so proud of her sweater stretchers,
mindless in her giggly titty-prance,
    Sarah offers you grace.
The spent man, slumped with regret,
seeking some salvation in baptismal gin —
    the night singer offers redemption.
Small-souled man seeks gratification in being missed,
longs to be missed....by someone.
    The night singer says you matter.

And I sing back:
When the black-and-red rage of our disappointments
rings its revenge for sins undefined
we must have committed, but cannot remember
we cannot remember, 'cause we did them half- blind.

We beg the night singer to sing it so tender
for sins unremembered, sing it so kind,

for sins unremembered, sing us half- blind,
for sins unremembered, we're losing our minds,
they're still undefined....still undefined...
we're paying the price for sins undefined.

You whisper a promise to a room full of lovers
who're caressing each other with auras, not eyes.
There's the promise. Always the promise;
we're lured by the promise, to the end of the line.
I fear I'm unworthy — I must not be worthy,
I must not be worthy — the sin's now defined.

Trudging the gauntlet of my chains and chores,
I can't seem to ease the ice in my throat.
My hunger had shrunk and faded away.
My once lurking wolf stopped stalking and sulked,
unsteeled, mystified, that his fires had died.

To my brandy-embracing small table,
she bids me *Cling to the promise.*
Don't be "Sad Thomas," doubting your wounds.
I find you are worthy, you've always been worthy.
I'll tend your illness with the words in my tunes

She's a gifted mystic with her lyrical skills.
She sings to us like passing out pills.

We ask the night singer, "What is the answer?"
"To what?" she replies, disappointing us dear.
"The answer *is* there" she assures us quite calmly,
"but only when the *question* is clear."

In a room we all sit in a distant dimension,
we become a mirage in a world without time;
it began with our first drink, and the suspension
ends on the street with the door closing behind.

Scenes That Strike You Silent

Did you, my friend, there alone in your dark,
ever wish you could spark the soul of another
with scenes you believed you alone saw,
but feared your call would go unheard?

The lines down below, are for you to know
that world-wide we sit in a dark of our own;
fearing our calls, too, might go unheard.
It's really a shame, and almost absurd.

I
You wish you could have said something
to the parents who tend, and then depart;
to fade like the dust of papers in some
                              forgotten attic.
And only their caressing eyes
remain in your mind
to appear in quiet moments — like angels — and
                                make you ache.

II
And during the daily march of your existence,
when, with a word, a song, a scene in a park,
came the memory of a woman — and you grew still.

III
You heard some haunting piano refrains
curling across a midnight city
under a lightly blowing snow
swirling in empty streets.

IV

Or wishing you could retreat years back
to some golden place in your youth,
only to find there, a rusty gate
                        creaking in the wind.

V

Remember when you wandered off
and sat alone by the tree,
wishing that someone special had searched
you out and stood behind you? You turned,
                        but no one was there.

VI

Or were you once freezing in a midnight street,
crushed by the immensity of a tall black city,
wondering if the night would ever end?

VII

Or with rain falling endlessly under a street lamp
you didn't know which direction to turn
                        with empty arms.

VIII

Did you see the snow drift against the frosty
country fence below the world's highest sky
in the silence that made time stand still?

IX

Do you cultivate a memory
and fight its fading
      it's so sweet
            and crushing
                  by its beauty
                        and tragic swiftness
or its pain exaggerated by time?

Those lines I've just shown are for you to know
that world-wide we sit in a dark of our own;
fearing our calls, too, might go unheard.
It's really a shame, and almost absurd.

I Would Fight More Fiercely

I would fight more fiercely
if the years would take me back.
Not view my yard more clearly
but hold more dearly
      the hunters' hedgerow
      and magic diamonds in my sack.

I would hold with daring deeds,
the wispy golden girls spellbound.
Not lure them with seeking seed
nor feast upon my aching needs
      the idolizing girls
      but love their wispy laughter's sound.

I would dream more wildly
if this child would tarry here.
Not to grow up mildly
but joyous and excited,
      that shining time
      and dare to "yes" those sparkling years.

I would fight more fiercely
if the years would take me back.
Not view my yard more clearly
but hold more dearly
      those golden years which are
      the magic diamonds in my sack.

Blessing Space

In a society of advanced technology, the very air we breathe is thick with expectations. The population paces in anticipation of taking the next step closer to Utopia. One might conclude that technological endeavors bespeak a shallow arrogance; and even though I agree that that aspect exists, I think the *compulsion* to discover exists independently of the desire for sudden wealth or deification.

Everyone has heard that if a man built a warehouse, he could not force himself to leave any part of it vacant. Man cannot ignore capacity. It is a physical and metaphysical impossibility to resist being drawn into a vacuum. If an answer is knowable, then goddamnit, we want to know it.

A common comment, "Why are we spending millions of dollars in space exploration when there are millions of people on this planet literally starving to death?"

My answer is this: If the number of starving people doubled what it is now, or if the cost of space exploration doubled what *it* is, it wouldn't change anything. If exploration proponents completely ran out of contrived excuses, and there were no practical value whatsoever to going out there, we would go. We cannot *not* go.

The mountain climber who explained, "We climb that mountain because it's *there*," answered correctly. Everyone knew there was nothing up there to justify climbing to its cold and brutal top.

Outer space may offer the answers to some important questions about our planet—some relevance to our existence, but even if it did not, it would not change anything. We're going. Whatever exists, must be touched by us—"blessed" by us. Not necessarily in arrogance. Maybe even with humility, or in reverence, like the shaky hand that finally touched the top of Mt. Everest. The humanly-touched thing.

Rocks and dust, dead as dirt, surrounding a tiny sprig of clover, tiny in its green promise, need only sit with patience. As sure as life, the clover will reach out its diminutive tentacles — indomitably and unquestioningly — to touch the dead dirt and "bless" it. Likewise, the astronaut will risk it all to bless the black, dead silence with the living. Blackness, more expansive than the human mind can grasp, will be invaded by the strangest sound ever heard in that cold….breathing.

Lazarus on a Spur Line

An abandoned boxcar on a spur line,
its dejected, broad shoulders
beaten into submission by
wind, dust, and showers...
      the seasons.

Its steel and planks, dead as Mars
collect invisible Spring debris.
Streaks of mud run down its once
      worshipped face.

Naps of mud gather on its sagging roof
Spring upon Spring.
Now, without fanfare, a tiny, yellow
blossom lifts its baby face to the wind,
its roots cling green to those dying
      rust shoulders.

In time-without-numbers, sibling
blossoms crawl rampant,
conquering the crumbling, dead steel.
In ages, the transformation will be complete.
Left only will be a mound of
green and yellow life. Indiscriminate life;
undefeatable;
      inexplicable;
            inexplicable;
                  inexplicable.
Lazarus on a spur line.

Self-Improvement Books

I prowl the book racks
to fill in the cracks
that my bland environ done left me.

Incomplete, insecure
there's one thing I'm sure,
a know-it-all author can help me.

To complete my perfection
and my resurrection
a search for *the* book I do strive.

I'll find I'm embarrassed
When standing in line,
With all that perfection
For twelve ninety-nine.

To Loren Eiseley
(as a man nearly seventy, recalls riding a freight-car in his twenties)

On a rushing train rustling leaves
riding in the warm whipping wind
in the world's most perfect morning.

Lying flat on the black boxcar
in a glistening September countryside
passed fields and leaves and side-roads.

On impulse he waved at a girl
in a red roadster stopped by the tracks,
and prettily she waved back.

He knew he would never see her again.
Everything was moving: The train,
the wind, the leaves, the season — time.

He waved 'til the train rounded a curve.
There was no turning back. It was brief,
loving, touching, heart-stabbing — "Times Arrow."

He wondered where she was going
in that car. He wonders where
she is now — half a century on.

He wonders if she recalls time itself
rolling by and the man clinging
to the freight-car top.

Time, he thinks: Either you ride away
on its back or stop and it goes
by you with someone else on it
that you'll never see again,
                waving farewell.

And some of us, Loren, long past
rounding the curve, keep waving
        and waving
                until we feel foolish
                    and alone
                            and drop our hands.

Alaskan Winter Night

Sneaking out of dark windy streets,
voices seeping out of yellow windows,
and gravel crunching under my feet,
I treat the night with quiet passing.

Wood smoke leaves the stacks
of shacks, circles the houses
upon its back,
slips off into the night and disappears.

The night so cold it could crack,
the spruce so black it hurts,
alder smoke so sweet and white
lies heavily on the hills.

And wrapped in the presence of one another,
those inside utter things not required
to be said or heard to know
they are there in communion with time
                                      and each other.

Old Cordova

Alaska in Summer

Movies make people think that geographical regions have personalities. I always thought that the South looked like the South, like *Fried Green Tomatoes*, or the swelter of Tennessee William's pen. I thought that a small town in Kansas was the color of wheat, silos baking in the sun, a sleeping old dog on the sidewalk. In truth, all these things exist only in the memory of Norman Rockwell. In truth, these regions are interchangeable, and geographically unrecognizable. Just the way our over-analyzing benefactors want it: clean and controllable. The spirit of the supermarket, (that homogenous extension of psychoanalyzed people)...stainless surfaces...packaged commodities...or ranch homes...interchangeable, and geographically unrecognizable. A town is really one, long, strip mall.

By contrast, summer in old Cordova was what one would expect: exciting. When the fishing fleet returned to town for the weekend, it was an invasion. Main Street's two- and three-storied wooden buildings — built shoulder to shoulder — bristled with activity. The huge canneries — heavy timber and corrugated sheet steel — perched on trestles of creosoted pylons high above the water, roared with work, under clouds of steam and swirls of squawking and diving gulls. It all came with the fishermen in wool jackets, hip boots rolled down below the knees, tousled hair, faces red from wind, hands like hams, suspenders, loud voices, the smell of fish and diesel fuel. The bars bellowing laughter, roaring curses and tumbling wooden chairs, scooted tables, clacking pool balls, 45-gallon garbage cans filling up with empty beer bottles, one after another. Even the weekly City Council meetings started with a curse, a fist-fight, followed by the Pledge of Allegiance.

For God's sake, don't tell the urban social analyzers, they'll come up and try to "fix" it.

On the Docks

Standing still in misty wind,
listen…the gulls call above
the boats rocking gently
on the docks.

The harbor sea sleeps and sways
gently in her dreams,
in the afternoon haze as gray
and cool as the dew upon my coat.

I hear no voice break the mist,
no boot creak upon the dock,
and only the wind is there
to spray my face and baptize my mind.

My years stand still this day,
my mind as clear as Sunday bells,
wrapped a moment in every solitude
I ever built and locked around myself.

The Sailor and the Whore

Scene 1

The sailor...
Strutting out of steaming R 'n B's, the thumping bass
and stiletto "snick," passed evil glares and violent
dares to put it on the line, he staggered down the
    broken street, snow sullen.
The sidewalks rolled to his embellished
    sea-legged swagger.
He bellowed chanteys like he didn't care,
    pretending he was Welsh.
No one was ever so alone.
Inside, hollow as a kettle drum, the echoing hurt his
    heart.
What had he done to knock his life as flat as piss?
He knew the echoes would drum him to his end.

The whore...
Pacing snow-crunch, shivering in time to the
street-long thumping bass steaming from the R 'n B's;
the mean curses and breaking glass down the block,
    floated to her snowy corner.
She hummed a love song with cold, cracking notes,
    pretending she was loved.
Inside, shaking like a tambourine, jingling her jangling
    heart.
Shooting "H" had knocked her life as flat as piss
    And marked the trail to her vein-swollen end.

Scene 2

They connected with nods through foggy breaths;
feigned smiles like they really gave a shit.

Nothing is what it is
and where it is, ain't here.
No one is who they really are
as they climb the creaking stairs.

This whore who had watched
through the whispering years
her love pumped away;
love in the frost, lost
to the crystallined silence
a hundred times before
half-spent mornings dragged her up.

Does she dare to drift back
to a dream of her own,
to the fabled Cinderella nailed now to the wall?
That simple, lovely, Cinderella,
who, years before this stranger,
honestly felt that oxen had knelt
      before the manger,
has since loin-hammered
nails in Mary's coffin.

With breasts pressed by nameless chests
she had grown hard
like the bride widowed
a dozen times a night.

Please deliver me, she sighed,
from inside this room,

soiled and spoiled by the stench
of a hundred drunken nameless grooms.

But she does not fear
the devil in her groin
and lying down numb and deep
spreads resigned to the approaching wave
with her virtue toppling and burning
with every humping hero
in the crucifixion of her womb.

But in the sailor's mind, the lilting bride
would rise with him by the cabin fires
warm and lit in the light of their love;
curled in the furled flesh of their needs,
their breaths as warm as desert winds,
they'd stroll through the days of meadows.

And in their minds, the pictures built,
the bride and groom melt'd
in the surging search
as she arched and swelled
under his finger-tipping strokes,
they kissed to nick their lips
on the thorn of the rose.

She tried to forget
with whispers and sighs,
there's another mad Hamlet
there in her thighs.

The groom and bride in a life-time hour
witnessed and celebrated their common dreams;
as the door to her desire glided wide
and entered the Spring lion
with mane-flaring fierceness

that bellowed and bounded
and roared in his flaming need
as wild as burning horses on the plains.

The savage sailor aflame
to fill the space left gaping
spin in violent compensating
to careen into the well
and light off lightning.

"Oh, whatever sin, spin us here,
to ignite genesis upon these sheets,
to light this room and ignite our souls.
Oh, for the moment bless us
in this fierce need —
until the climatic blood
warns of the coming flood!"

He kept her warm and alive
in the embers of his love —
in the needing sheets
In the flesh-wet center of the world.

His lips in her hair, wrapped there
in each others mirage,
love held them bound and bowed and blessed.

Scene 3

Well...
In the dark, in the room,
the love forsaken, abandoned there:
And in the street, the pair unpaired
neglecting to mourn the widow's loss.

Shuffling on down the broken street,
the Welshman swaggered his "all is well"
toward his flat-as-piss sunrise—
    Unconvincing fellow.
And the widow thumbed her crumpled cash
for the serum that makes
    the sun rise in her hollow.

To Dr. Francis Scheaffer

I wonder what moves this man
about the countryside
through Swiss meadows
or medieval streets of European towns.

This man as tender as a leaf
or Irish oxen hard and straight
whose heart glows as voices spent
centuries ago.

As voices quest'd in volumes bound
in leather as old as man's mind —
to seek substance for their kind in this
whirring time of stressed despair.

This Irish-oxen leaf throughout
his time consoled Plato's soul
and eased the pain Picasso felt
when contradicting his own brush.

When Kirkegaard and Sartre
pulled apart the rug from
under mankind's feet and urged
the existential leap to blackness;

this tender man with tender
voice calmed the seas
within their souls
and said, "You do exist."

And said, "God's children please be calmed"
in abstract terms as real as leaves
and zen-like trees did silently
wait his words.

But far more real than leaves and trees
or Plato's stumbling split-souled man,
are children lost upon their knees
in answerless and aimless dread.
It pulls this tender man's heart
down, the children's
desperate searching quest
for values in the volumes read.

But those who listen to his voice like leaves
and see the light shine from his eyes
are beacon-drawn like ships in seas
to quiet ports where all things lie.

Crossing the Line
(Speaking of Schaeffer)

Let's stretch the science vs. art topic a little further. How about science vs. religion or philosophy? I was reading Dr. Francis Schaeffer's *Escape From Reason*, in which Schaeffer traced the evolution of certain aspects of Western philosophy. Before jumping into his first example—Thomas Aquinas' *Suma Theologica*—he drew a horizontal line across the page. Below the line, he wrote "particulars," and above the line, he wrote "universals." Well, actually, he wrote "nature" below the line and "grace" above the line, but I'm modifying it a bit because he's dead, so I can get away with it. Anyway, using that approach, Leonardo—the real one—placed a lot of faith in his below-the-line particulars—his studies of mathematics, or engineering, or anatomy—wanting to discover some higher, more universal meaning in them. Not finding any, he thought that if he could create a connection between them, that new view might reveal a higher meaning. But, you know, math is nothing but "particulars." Using mathematics, you only end up with machines. Pretty astounding machines, for sure, but just machines. Man is viewed as a machine when one believes he is a "blank slate" engineered by tricks and chemistry and gimmicks. Eugenics promises to be the ultimate "machinist" who will be able to rummage down our DNA of mentality and character to a common (and then modifiable) denominator; subjecting it to our natural need to "fix it" (human flaws, that is). In the meantime, here we all sit in our collective Columbine cafeteria, hoping our machinists can tinker away the quiet rage of our assassins before lunch time.

You know, sitting below the line is the world of reason. The world of the rational. "But on the basis of all reason, man is meaningless," writes Schaeffer. As such, you have what Heiddegger called Angst. Angst is not just fear, because fear has an object. Angst is a vague feeling of dread. Existentialism is a dead-end street leading to hollow emptiness.

I'm sure, to save his "soul," Leonardo occasionally pole-vaulted himself above the line and into the arts. But the "universals" there were hard to quantify logically, and his logical mind could not tolerate that. Scientists may delve below a man's DNA yet never comprehend a man's kind act of selflessness. Selflessness is neither scientifically identifiable nor logically defensible. For those who believe a man is more than what is seen, (packaged in his skin and directed by that synapse-snapping command post—located, sub-divided, and categorized by the Sagan-babbling technicians) then, they must soar above the line, in the domain of the "universals," only to see an even wider variety of foggy possibilities. There, our map-less explorers cross paths with theologians of every conceivable denomination, who are as self-assured as their scientific counter-parts below the line. Also drifting above the line are those artists and their misty-eyed groupies anguishing over some conclusion they would like to reach about the "specialness" of Man.

Dan Brown's "Leonardo"—the priest/physicist—was someone who apparently lived on both sides of the line; someone who might be able to poke a hole in the line allowing the two worlds to merge. The real Leonardo could not do it. Dan Brown had his Leonardo whacked before he—Brown—had to explain how it is done.

Another thing that Schaeffer mentioned was that the below-the-liners will always devour the above-the-liners. Below-the-liners have the best tools. With their scientific devices, their data-collecting and formula-producing computers, they can validate and prove everything. Nothing ethereal is provable. Above-the-liners can only appeal to man's soul without being able to prove the soul exists.

In walks John Edward and Sylvia Brown. The place goes so silent you can hear the scientist drop his test-tube. The sociologist guards his pie-chart, and the theologians pray and light incense. Oh, this is gonna be good.

John says, "I'm getting a message from someone who has passed." The technocrats roll their eyes. Sylvia adds "Yep, I see him. He had red hair, didn't he?" The theologians hang garlic around their necks and start chanting incantations.

Alternately, John and Sylvia poke holes in Schaeffer's line. Leonardo sits up and starts taking notes. Kahlil Gibran starts strumming a zither. All the Buddhists start nodding, "I told you so."

No, let me say it another way.

An old friend, Baptist minister Richard Harding, asked me if I'd seen the movie, *The Matrix*? I said, "No." He got all excited and insisted I see it. He explained the general plot to me. He explained that computers had taken over the world but they needed to be fed to live. So people were kept alive, but comatose, in cocoons while waiting their turn to be eaten. Yet, while the humans were in these cocoons, wires were attached to them through which sensations were fed to these comatose people. The people were electronically injected with illusions of living normal lives—working, raising families, etc. They did not realize that their individual lives were an illusion. Except a few. These few—rebels—had escaped the "Matrix" and were hiding out while waiting to rebel against it. They were waiting for "The One" that would some day arrive and lead the rebellion. They were waiting for this individual because an oracle had predicted his coming.

So, I rented the movie, and it was cool. The characters in the movie had interesting names. Lawrence Fishburn was the rebel leader who had been searching for "The One"—like a Messiah—to arrive, train, then lead the rebellion. Fisherburn's character's name was "Morpheus." His female partner was "Trinity." Keanu Reeves—The One—was "Neo." The turncoat, the Judas, of the movie, was "Ishmia." Morpheus (process of change), and Trinity (all together), located Neo (new) and trained him. Ishmia (like Ishmael, son of Abraham, and root word for Ismaelite meaning "outcast"), performed what I thought was the key scene in the movie. Ishmia contacted the agents of the Matrix and told them that he would deliver Neo to them in exchange for a favor. Real reality was tedious, boring, uncertain, and all-around unpleasant for Ishmia. He wanted to go back into the Matrix. Be plugged in again. He didn't care that the electronically contrived reality was an illusion. It was better. During a secret meeting with an agent, Ishmia was eating a steak. He remarked that he knew that there really was no steak in front of him. He knew that his brain was being injected with the sensation of the tender and tasty meat. And he said he didn't care. It was better than the real gruel he had been eating in reality. Besides — what's the difference? In an attempt to improve life, we often get a contrived, engineered, no-risk imitation of it.

When Neo met up with the rebels, Morpheus explained to Neo that the Matrix had been a programmed illusion and offered Neo a choice. He held out both hands. In one hand was a blue pill and in the other was a red pill. He explained that taking the blue pill would allow Neo to return to the Matrix and never remember he had visited reality. The Matrix was a known.... contentment until the time of oblivion. But, taking the red pill would make him a part of the rebel group. It would be similar to following Alice down the rabbit hole to possibilities like risks, adventure, boredom, uncertainty, or disillusionment. There were no guarantees following the rabbit. Of course, Neo took the red pill. Plucky guy.

Consider this: "reality" is only what's registered in the brain electronically and deciphered or interpreted. Once I heard an example cited: If you were on a camping trip and could not be contacted from home, and unbeknownst to you, a loved one died, would you feel sad? Of course not. So, it's not the loved-one's dying that causes you grief. The death occurred. It was real. But it is only when your mind perceives it that you mourn. "Reality" is what is injected into your mind. Not what really is.

Well, of course Neo won the battle, not because he was Neo, but because he was Keanu Reeves for Chrissakes. Had the epoch continued, I wonder if the human race he saved from certain ignorant oblivion would have loved him, or would they have hated him because he threw them into a life of uncertainty followed by its eventual — and anticipated — oblivion?

Wait....is oblivion a certainty? We know that things exist all around us that cannot be perceived directly by our brains. We believe that atoms are real. We are so certain, that our science is based on something that can be conceived but not perceived. Some of these things — light, sound, mass — are only close enough to our perception range to be detectable by these fabulous machines we live in. Still, an astonishing amount of "reality" is beyond what our senses — our machines — can detect. What lies below our DNA? What "thing" is our universe only a small part of? What lies below or above what we can conceive of? In fact...what are we?

Echoing archeologist Loren Eiseley, "Where in me do I live?" If I'm made up largely of carbon, can the carbon be drawn out, and find that "I" reside in it? Is it in the water? Is it in the brain — and if so, what part? If biologists are correct, that in a seven-year span, every cell in your body has died and is replaced by a brand new one, why do you still have a memory? Where are these images stored? How are they passed from a dying cell to a new one? Were nineteenth century science fiction buffs correct, that if my brain were placed inside another person that he would become me, or I him? Is seventeenth century philosopher, John Locke correct; is everyone born a blank slate who becomes ultimately — and only — what his/her life has written on that slate? Or, are others correct who maintain that people have a neurological imprint at birth? Am "I" contained in any form of mass at all? Are solids, liquids, and gasses the only forms of mass that exist? Will our fabulous instruments someday expand on these insights? Will someday, some incredibly innovative Kirlian photographer be able to photograph an otherwise invisible vaporous mass rising up from a dying person and proclaim he photographed the soul leaving the body? Will other skeptical scientists smugly inform him he only captured a death fart? Will John Edward, sitting alone in a warehouse, agree to pose for a "group" photo?

But is mass the only thing that exists? I'm including the mass that is beyond our perception or what can be conceived. What about concepts? Good? Evil? Are they only contrived for the convenience of social man?   Are there levels of existence or levels of consciousness running simultaneously and invisibly linked? Is God a reality only to those who can conceive of such and cannot exist independently of their willingness to believe? Can something that big be accurately explained to mass-man by a hillbilly wearing a cheap pastel suit and sporting an immaculate pompadour, who likes to pace as he pontificates? I love to watch these guys when they get so intense, they burst into tears and sob uncontrollably. Actually, the coolest ones are the southern, black Baptist ministers. If you drive around the south, spin your radio dial, you never have to be without a sermon. The southern, black Baptist ministers are the last bastion of great, American oratory. I love to watch these guys on TV. Those huge chocolate figures in pin-striped suits with color-coordinated handkerchiefs for wiping the floods of sweat as they bellow and roar in baritone, then spike up to a contralto range with that black gravelly rasp so pronounced it makes B.B. King sound white. Watching them on TV, I get really pumped up. But, as cool as they are, are they qualified to explain what is highest above the line?

Of course, one could be an atheist. But even atheists are cultural Christians—all the benies without the commitment. Cool. The neat thing about that is that the atheist doesn't have to start from scratch to develop a list of "goods" and "bads." Getting the answers to these questions only requires being patient. I'm sure Keanu Reeves will be along shortly.

Actually, I found the answer. Well—I didn't find it,

some physicists did. These three guys won the Pulitzer Prize in physics in 2004 with "The String Theory" (the theory of everything). In it, they resolved the dilemma that Einstein struggled with but didn't have time to resolve. He couldn't swallow the idea that there were two separate theories – one for space and one for energy. One for "out there" and another one for "in here." Well, the string theory resolved that problem, but while at it, illustrated something else interesting. Prior to "strings," we were limited to Time, plus three dimensions (left-right, back-forth, up-down). Well, sort of. But right after the discovery of these little curls and wads of "strings," these guys discovered that there were actually five dimensions. They never got so far as to surmise what might be "in" the extra two dimensions, though. Well, now they are up to eleven dimensions. Dimensions? Holy shit! If below-the-line physicists are trying to substantiate and locate above-the-line dimensions, John Edward and Sylvia Brown found a new batch of drinking buddies. Of course, nobody knows what's in these other dimensions. But John and Sylvia think they know what's in a couple of them: All my dead relatives are in one, but more important, my favorite screw driver that inexplicably disappeared in 1973 is in another. Now, I have vowed that the first thing I'm going to do when I die, is to go to that dimension and get all my shit back.

Look, I know it's a bit of a stretch to surmise that the String Theory might poke some holes in Schaeffer's line dividing Nature and Grace, or Science and Religion, but there's nothing wrong with pondering stuff. Right?

A Few Yards Short of a Poem

To him, one gray morning was so much like another in the sea-sided town, still and steel-cold under the Alaskan frost. The wooden buildings sat rickety and rigid under the icy sky, and the town behind him lay layered in the lake-swept wood smoke stoked by the stumbling early risers. Out of his earshot, the cups rattled in the cupboard, the sounds of coffee leaving the spout, stout as the bewhiskered mug-clutchers blearily welcoming the morning that arrived with the sound of a creaking board.

He strolled past one early riser stiffly laden with stove logs, stomping at the cold, clench-jawed in his frost and smoking breath, and his dog, jolly and jumping against its chain.

And looking back he saw the air-borne ice crystals blown and tumbling down the mountainside like mad Vikings storming a huddled and hover-shouldered hamlet which lies frozen in time. The ice fog — wind at its heels — weaved, ducked, tumbled through blue spruce whose stoic, Noah-old stance remained unbent before the onslaught.

>   Cold and still
>   Bleak wintry dot
>   Against the hill
>   Had time begot
>   Furless creatures
>   Huddled there
>   Fragile features
>   And fragile bare?

Descending on to the stinging bay, he watched the boats rise and fall minutely, nod and knock the thump of wood: Heard the rigging creak like deserted warehouses. Those hulls — shaped by the hands of Neptune — as evolution trimmed and skinned, keel-sharp, the birds that fly the currents of the sea.

Weather shined, the wind-blown whale wanderers white with winter icing lie hibernatingly sleepy, like bears who shudder slowly awake in the Spring. Lifelessly moored, blank and black windows stared back—desolate as dead factories.

And down the cannery bay looming wood and tin, pylon-high, history-old, the final graveyard of fishes in cans: The ultimate insult for death-defying, predator-dodging, wide-eyed and nose-led salmon who run head-long toward their own oblivion—of one sort or another—and, insult of insults, never knowing they were born to die only.

But, oh, to be swept and cradled in the engulfing blue, weightless and diving, soaring and plunging, or just drifting sleepily in unseen and benevolent hands and never know they were born to die only.

But having seen the fish and gulls and wind-sliced winter water lapping salt and ice and mud and shells; and having heard the gulls call the seven seas to shore and hull, to pylon-high, cold and echo-empty buildings, he moved on down the beach line.

Wandering up the narrow slough, crunching through the low-tide ice on mud, past the turn-of-the-century boat houses sagging plank and tin, perched up on green algae pylons with crusted muscles blue and dead—the smell of salt and ocean bottom. The structures, like ancient warriors dangling ribbons, medals and bandages, dangled remnants of rope, cable, net webs and floats. Peak-perching gulls gathered facing the wind above a skulking cat discreet upon a sway-bracing. The pale sun, shyly out, glinted off cracked crystal windows.

He nodded at old John who was busy with some obscure task. Gray coated and fray cuffed, John, hands gnarled with time and salt—veins like small ropes—waved back....barely. Then John, odored like wet wool and tobacco, bent back to his purpose.

Ascending the far side he looked up at the hill's peak

which lords over the town and the track to follow which permeates the spruce and blown crystals to the cold, smoking top. Absently wondering why he should climb, he climbed. Up through the brush and passing day he ascended solitary even to not speaking to himself. Leaving further behind and more faint the town's growing morning sounds of door-slamming children, rock-clacking, twig-snapping, hooded and mufflered mini-terrors in mismatched mittens dashing between houses and sheds.

Forty years to the day of his birth he sought the mountain top. Ascending the encasing gray, he pounded back the forty years with long strides denying their ache.

At the top, the cold wind, dwarfing the dinosaurs' bones, sang the song it began when God first flashed lightning across the sky; when first the thunder fell on ears not yet born; when first the seas rolled over the highest peaks and galaxies ignited in wracks beyond all imagination—for that long, the same wind blew. For that long the wind dusted this peak and blew a millennia of foliage created, expired, and bedded down, age upon age, layer upon layer, until the ground became the frozen sponge upon which he stood now to count his two-score life.

> High and bold
> Wind and cold
> Utter a language
> A millennia old

On the cold windy crest there are none of those things to busy oneself in order to take no note of Time. Time, though quiet, is always just over one's shoulder, so that in moments of solitude and reflection one merely needs to turn around to feel its dusty breath upon one's face. Time, which disappears with laughter, work, or worry, nuisance that it is, creeps back to breathe upon one's neck just when one forgot it existed.

Yet, here, now, Time (in that petty sense)—muscle and skin, heart and lung, and the vanity of humanistic desires for immortality—blew like the ice crystals over the edge. Because, he, shaking off Time, had climbed this peak to celebrate and to feel the wind. The wind is old, man's soul is older. And the wind that spoke to the pre-ice reptiles, speaks to him now, and in turn will speak to solitary celebrators eons from now.

> If within the living web of cells
> Lies reason unreasonably clear,
> If all is written and pre-set
> Then useless effort is our fear.

Glancing down to sea and town, with honest awe, he salutes mankind's mad migration from tropics to this. Truly, the Creator created creatures who create: Creatures who play "winner-take-all" with the elements…who make habitable the scrubs, boulders, ice, and marsh. What arrogance and dash to plant into hostile climates whole empires whose very existence depends upon wooden boxes within which they must live—to live. What grit, to yank the wind's tail by placing a wooden box in its path, then cast a dare to blow it down. Done? Fine. We'll build another. Another yank: Blow a fool-hardy fisherman to his doom in a swollen, raging sea. We will mourn, toast, and send another, who with cap cocked cockily and pipe blazing fiercely, will bludgeon into the fish-filled storm to fight tooth and nail with nature for the right to coexist. And true, the sea's surge can wipe a town from its rocks, but before Neptune can catch his breath, hammers and nails will ring across the countryside.

But still, here, on this high hill, the wind speaks in confidence and celebration. And the wind will speak to solitary celebrators eons from now: Whether they be one-candled cake clutchers; or torn, toothless and limping old soldiers of life meagerly managing one last celebration; or the mid-way traveler, half-way home.

> Mid-way traveler, half-way home
> Descend the slope at a natural pace,
> Pharaoh's father tread the path
> That each new man himself shall face.

To Don

I seem to see him today
                as clearly as ever
in the fields behind the barn,
a happy, yellow, grass-hopper chaser;
a stumbling bundle of blond boyhood
kicking up pollen and
terrifying field mice.

He was a chubby, red-cheeked
little round thing wearing
tennis shoes and rampaging the fields
under the summer sun.

When sometimes
in the morning, he would venture out
to the dew-covered fields
to sneak up on crickets.

Or at times lie
        down on his stomach
and swear he could hear
crickets crashing through dew drops
like soldiers through mud.

      *   *   *

With the winds blowing across the fields
in that sun-sparkling day,
the mornings were shot with gold.
The vast green and golden plain
lay baking like a sleeping dog
lazy in the mid-day haze.

The sun-flushed earth could burst
from its swelling silence,
save the sound of a far-off tractor
somewhere in the dizzying distance.

Beneath the endless suspended sun
he spun rocks at the scarecrow
staring silently by the dusty fence.

Or he would stare and dream
until the sun loomed low
and the long shadow of that statue
reached the road.

       *   *   *

Yet, they came:
The days of wine and vile vermouth
that lay still in the still of his youth,
when he dreamed he would
knightly charge time and life
for the favors of immortality —
to be unseated by his own years.

Yet they came:
The heartbreak, the joys, the challenging world,
the seed sent searching in the
rustling bushes with
girls giggling in their games;
the creation relived day by day
in the Eden of his years
and not the fear of the coming frost
that bends the wintry winds
in the days further down the road,

where he'd turn to meet himself
walking down a dusty road
and dare to ask how far he's going
and which fork it is
        to the end.

The girls, the names, the games,
the star-lit back seat sighs,
the wines, the songs, the lines
poetically read, under the endless circling
of the stars.

The meet, the match, the win, the loss,
the cross of reality strapped
to his back, the sack in which
he carried his youth;
truths of his life
        dropped by the tracks.

      *   *   *

You can return, Don, only to find
dust upon the banisters.
To return to the years of the sun-shot days
is worse than a reverse-laid street,
it's a hole, not unlike a grave,
the brave escape from which
is a bitch to say the least,
and it lies dead east
        of your Eden.

Life, my friend, is a one-way street,
straight ahead where I hope you'll meet
yourself with a sack upon your back
filled with your strength, the
full length of your soul.

The fields are still there,
the house and the barn,
the scarecrow still looms
its shadow down low,
it pains me as much
as it pains you I know
there's still only one direction to go.

It's senseless, my friend,
        to be who you are,
Unless you intend
        to be who you are.

Saturday Mornings

The breeze-danced sun-streams
land solid on the cluttered kitchen table,
surrounded by tousle-haired children
with all of creation in their eyes
      and crumbs in their laughter.

They burst forth from slamming screen doors
to conquer the mountains of their minds
and destroy the villains of innocence
with shrieks and shouts and urgency
      and swords of sticks at the ready.

Victorious at sunset, the conquering warriors return.
The porch is strewn with armaments —
broken sneakers, twisted caps, jelly-stained jackets.
The villains of innocence were held at bay
      for one more Saturday

Sadat

He walked with the dignity of a
kingdom as old as the written word.

The goodness and figure of a father,
he died under the sighs of the pharaohs.

The sacrificing Christ of his convictions,
unflinching, faced the lions of his legions.

Hiroshima

Frankenstein's inhuman monster was made of human parts. No single part was guilty of terror: No eye, no arm, no leg. The terror was in the uncontrollable totality of its parts.

Little men with bated breath searched for uranium like an Easter egg hunt. Not guilty. Annihilation in a laboratory smock, white as snow, cold as stone, hovered over by a snap-brimmed army, gray as bone, each man detached from the end of the scheme. Each was innocent...*system* cleansed.

Guiltless drones: Each just a fiber in the hangman's rope. Yet none did trip the trap, nor heard the rap of the Nuremberg gavel. With instruments of stainless steel, death was assembled like a puzzle, each piece—an eye, an arm, a leg. What is the square root of horror?

Above the Japs, the red-buttoned thumb cross-haired humanity to kill a samurai by an equation; to obliterate by the crank of a handle; a trigger pulled from a cushioned chair. A bell-toll of finality. Okay.

The round demon, Enola's egg, hung suspended, gape-mouthed—a silent scream—as though by the grace of God, it

would.....
    not.....
        fall.....
            on.....
                children.

Hold tight, little black-eyed darlings, in your barefoot and silk, your mud pies on the steps, as Satan's sun hangs soundless above you. Pit-pat around in your baggy pants from your nap, then stand, poised, open-mouthed with your words split in mid-breath. Snap the muffled chant of children's songs. The last thing you see is the toy in your hand.

Children stretched across the altar of our flaws, Abraham with his knife raised, could not hear God cancel the order. Who ever saw a *system* grieve?

Introduction to "Reflections of Pontius Pilate"

I've had readers insinuate that my poem "Reflections of Pontius Pilate" is obscure. To me, obscure lines are like "If my head hurt a hare's foot, pack back the downed bone," and numerous other things written by Dylan Thomas. Nevertheless, I guess I expect others to automatically know what was in my head when I wrote things like "Reflections." I agonized over this poem because there were so many dimensions in that most fascinating epoch in history.

First, the relinquishing of personal liberties in exchange for security.

Next, the conflicting urges to give up national or ethnical identity in exchange for being annexed by a wealthy and powerful, but different culture.

Then I portrayed Pontius Pilate as the "politician caught in the middle." Later, I learned from the History Channel that Pilate was not the befuddled and impotent governor, but in fact was so heavy-handed that in putting down a subsequent insurgency he was too ruthless, even by Roman standards. Consequently, he was transferred to another area. But I refused to rewrite the poem.

It's hard for us to comprehend, but, the concept of "time" changed for all civilization after the onset of Christianity.

The most profound dimension was that the worth of a person is decreed by God, and cannot be modified even by the highest-ranking mortal.

And last, love replaced fear as an impetus for following divine rules.

I unintentionally noticed the contrast a few years ago, when I meandered through Ovid's *Metamorphoses*. I say "meandered" because Ovid's book on Roman (pagan) mythology didn't actually *go* anywhere. Like most folks, I expect to see either a "plot," moral, or at least a basic theme run through the books I read. I read like Diogenes in search of a point, but none was reflected in my meager light. The only common premise throughout was that the gods were all pricks. The gods were like a heavenly board of directors and Jove (sometimes known as Jupiter) was the chairman of the board. He was an asshole. His wife, Juno, was mean-spirited. All the mortals in the book had one thing in common, they were victims of the toying gods. The gods were just like ordinary people, except bigger. Dr. Francis Schaeffer described them as "amplified humanity." I never read any references to concepts of "good," or "justice," or "decency." There were no standards upon which one might find a footing. Life wasn't really even a game. A game must have at least some rules and a point to it all. Roman Emperor Augustus wasn't a big fan of the book, either. Right after its publication, Augustus ran Ovid out of town. The emperor believed that "Metamorphosis" might contribute to the downwardly spiraling moral fiber of the empire. Augustus was too late; his daughter and granddaughter were already humping half the Senate. Anyway, the monotheism of Abraham literally changed everything. But, I'm getting ahead of myself.

The willingness of frightened people to relinquish personal liberties in exchange for security was not new in those days and has changed little in the last two thousand years. In Rome itself, as well as its territories, the "mask of order" would drop by inches until gangs of toughs ran the streets and terrorized the meek. In Rome, that anarchy caused the Senate to appoint an iron-fisted Caesar. The Senate had to relinquish some of its power as a Republic (give up some of their democratic freedoms) in exchange for the feeling of security. When feeling frightened and vulnerable, individuals willingly gave up some of their personal freedoms to the iron-fisted ones who were strong enough to hammer the crap out of the armed gangs (vicious rogues) who roamed the midnight streets. So, Rome became an Empire, giving up its right to call itself a Republic. The Senators, wearing their red and white, could only pontificate their outrage at social anarchy, but lacked the collective balls to stop it. "By God, Caesar will stomp the snot out of them and make the streets safe again." They exalted in his power. They employed a hired gun and strutted in their confidence. He continued to demand more autonomous power to enable him to get the job done. They granted it, but each time feeling more uneasy about it. At first he was their guard dog, but later they feared he might "turn to take their throats." They began to fear the one they had recruited. Still, at his request, they made him Caesar for life and deified him. Later, they feared him so much they quietly plotted against his life.

The territories of Rome suffered similar problems. Areas which lost all law and order, petitioned Rome to come in and restore order.

Judea wanted to become a member of the Roman Empire. Most of Rome's neighbors did. That's where all the money was; the trade, the connections, it was the center of commerce and culture. But the Jews wanted to be an equal partner in the empire, not subordinate to Rome. Not all Jews thought that was a good idea. The Zealots wanted absolute independence and no affiliation with the Empire at all. They were "Libertarians." But the merchants and traders—the ones with money and influence— wanted to be Rome's fifty-first state. Sort of. Well they won their membership. The Zealots didn't like it and kept up attacks on Romans. Ever heard of Masada?

When an empire picks up a protectorate, it must appoint a governor. Judea was no exception. However, no one actively sought that position. Pontius Pilate was most likely a middle-management guy with obviously no friends of influence. Anyone with influential friends in the Roman Empire would not have got stuck with a tour of duty in Judea. No one in the empire—from soldiers to politicians—wanted to go to that nasty place with its obstinate, argumentative people, it's greedy merchants and fanatical zealots. Pilate was just some schmuck who was available and went. Pontius Pilate a sympathetic character? *I know that history must display my head upon a plate. But God told me He wrote no villains in that play.* There isn't much written about him afterwards. Except maybe he got stationed in Egypt for a while. He just disappeared into obscurity.

Even with the economic, cultural, and political turmoil, the Jews had a solid religion. It was very well established and a thousand years old. When theology is incorporated into an organized religion, or should I say, when a religion is organized into an institution, predictable manifestations occur. The Sadducees (ruling hierarchy, who believed only in the written law) hated the Pharisees (who were less anal). Then there was the local Jewish political/economic core group, the Sanhedrin, who tried to keep the peace—such as it was. So, in to the middle of this mess comes this little dusty, penniless rabbi from Nazareth.

Jesus had picked up a following and headed for Jerusalem. Jerusalem! What was he thinking? Did he have a death wish? Let's throw some gasoline on the fire. His promo crew thought it might be a great idea to announce that he…no, HE…was coming. How did he enter? The way that conquering generals or emperors would enter a conquered city, on a donkey. The humble donkey was used to show the citizens the general was just regular folks…a man of the people. So Jesus entered Jerusalem on a donkey after the crowds had been prepared by his advance-team. It was a well-thought-out production.

Well, the established clergy had seen their share of screwballs in the past. No big deal, except for one thing: Jesus headed for the temple, saw what was going on with the "money changers" and detonated. He demolished the place and ran them out. The temple was, in effect, the "establishment." The commerce of the money changers was a legitimate church enterprise. Actually, Jesus wasn't pissed about the commerce of selling sacrificial lambs, etc, but because of the corruption. The more affluent church-goers would pay top dollar for a quality lamb and be given some mangy lamb. Anyway, he ran them all out.

The "business" of the church was okay. And there was nothing wrong with the rituals and ceremonies of the church. After all, rituals are simply physical manifestations of mind-focusing. However, many of the wealthy worshippers paid top dollar hoping to buy their way into heaven. And the money changers were happy to soak them for the toll. Jesus felt the church's message was getting distorted. Jesus' message was new, but I guess his delivery was a little brusque. So, the outraged clergy went clamoring to the Sanhedrin to complain about this nut who claimed to be the messiah and wrecked the temple. The Sanhedrin, trying to keep the peace, (which in Judea was an impossibility) went to Governor Pilate.

But Jesus was a decent guy who, in Pilate's opinion, did nothing extreme enough to warrant crucifying. So Pilate tried a couple of ways of getting Jesus off the hook. If only Jesus would — well — *modify* what he said just a little, at least for right now, Pilate could let him go. Jesus stubbornly refused. No doubt about it, he had a death wish. *I offered him a hundred exits in the name of sanity and he stubbornly refused them all.* You know, if someone has a personal unique view, one could call it a philosophy. If one has a solid position, one could call it an ethic. But those positions are safe ones to take. The most they lead to are arguments. But a position that one would give one's life for....that's a morality. It's an ideal held so high, it is more important than your own life. *I see – morality does not exist until it becomes a liability to you.* Even the disciple Peter, buckled at this point. Peter was tough, spontaneous, and took no bullshit from anyone. In the garden, when the temple guards came to get Jesus, Peter jumped one of them and sliced his ear off. Yet after the crucifixion, when the mob was really pumped up, Peter denied being a follower....three times. His belief became too much of a liability. But I like Peter because he showed that he had flaws just like the rest of us. He was really just a blue-collar, neighborhood leader. He was the Bruce Springsteen of Galilee, a denim-wearing factory worker. He wore a robe with his bowling league embroidered on the back. They don't mention that in the Bible.

Jesus changed the world, literally. *Time* went from cyclical to lineal. It really began with the Christic perpendicular to the time-line of history. In all the previous cultures, history would only repeat itself forever. There was no game plan—no winners or losers—and most important no end of the game. It was like the tide going in and going out perpetually. "But He said the tides were counting." The tides were counting backwards. When it reached zero, it was all over. The Jews (and monotheism) initiated the point-tallying of a person's goods versus bads, but Jesus marked the countdown to the game's end.

Another major change: Jesus was not a hell-fire and brimstone rabbi. No other leader in history relied solely on being humble, gentle, kind and loving and stressed that this "Christ-like" approach as the way of improving the world. Before, it was fear and intimidation that was used. It was the most profound new approach...unbelievable. A new message: compassion and self sacrifice. A hippy...a Gandhi. In the early days, what attracted pagans to Christianity was their behavior. Groups of these Christians walked around tending to the sick. They visited prisoners, prayed with them, created a fellowship with them. They stressed morality and refused to have sex with children. Observers were stunned by the decency and compassion of these gentle people.

But most dramatic of all was that Jesus proclaimed that all persons were divinely bred. Aristocracies were humanistically contrived. Now, no leader could diminish the worth of even the lowliest person. Royal decree was immediately challenged. And it doesn't like that. If the Emperor expects to be regarded as a god himself, he would certainly resent this *nobody* from Nazareth un-deifying him. Rome was a very tolerant empire as far as religions went. The Romans didn't give a damn who or what one wanted to worship. There was only one condition: One must also worship or acknowledge Caesar as god as well. Simple. Except Jesus (and his followers) refused. Yep, *He marked an end when God was a welcomed guest at every table (providing God kept his opinions to Himself). The rabbi emptied banquet chairs across the world.* Love of your fellow man was born two thousand years ago on Golgotha. The concept of "humanity" did not exist before. Philosophically, tyranny cannot exist when "humanity" means all persons are of equal status, and no man—Caesar or not—can modify that. So Jesus *burned the scrolls that bore the mark of Caesar.*

If one contemplates Good Friday on an historical basis, it was the most dramatic world-changing event ever. What Man is may not be as important as what he believes himself to be. It doesn't really matter what theology one believes in. Even atheists are *cultural* Christians. The mind-set is irreversible and Western thought is what it is because of what happened one miserable April two thousand years ago.

Reflections of Pontius Pilate

The dusty April wind carried a tide of psalms
flooding the hills with the mark of mankind changing.

It was a time marked by bits of bloody flesh
stuck to the sole of the Roman sandal,
and the armor of their offer
to harmonize the cries for order.

Rome did what all mankind had begged
when first two beasts became neighbors,
when we angleworms fed off one another,
demonic conduct always laid
just beneath the mask of order.

The mask would drop by inches,
accepted by degrees,
until fear from every corner
rid night streets of decent men.

It was in Rome as before and since,
that when a horse-cart creaked
in a midnight street,
terror gripped the meek.

And our Senate outraged by vicious rogues
(their rhetoric stilled by sun-down)
indignant and determined, they knew
anarchy could not withstand that Roman fist
that left just pillars stand
where races were,
silent in the dawn of ages to come.

Oh, the white and red elegance —
the eloquence in the Senate Hall,

an episode they thought unique
is a pattern set in stone:
Remember —
**SOCIETIES DESPERATE FOR SOCIAL ORDER
PREFER THE SOUND OF THE SOLDIERS SWORD
TO THE UNCERTAIN STAMMER OF JUSTICE.**

We bred the Roman guard dog
and prayed it would not turn
to take our throats.

Tyrants don't force themselves upon us,
they are recruited and carried forward by our fears.
Ah, yes, the fearful are so easily led.
I had searched for perfection all my life
and believed it could be found
upon the scrolls above the mark of Caesar.

The history of tyrants is episodic:
In the dawn of their rule, we exalt in their power;
by noon — question it,
by dusk — fear it,
by nightfall — plot against it,
every horror real.
So it has been since the birth of the fist.

The history of history was episodic:
Prior to Him, life was the endless tide;
A day, a man, an empire — one like the next —
In, then out, an unconcluding succession of humanity,
done again and again;
promised to be such until the altar of mankind
eroded and blew away.

On foul-smelling afternoons, I would pass rows
of Jews suspended on poles

covered with dust and flies
rotting black and swollen
hideously under the pitiless sun —
and I hardly took notice at all.

And like the approach of another tide
— much like the day before —
rib-cage dogs, half shy, half mad
made attempts at men lashed
high above the ground
or licked the poles below,
and I hardly took notice at all.

Then He who said our worth was more
than royal decree
usurped the tablets that made legions move.
Oh God — He said the tide was counting!

He marked an end when God was a
welcomed guest at every table
(providing God kept his opinions to Himself).
The rabbi emptied banquet chairs across the world.
Still, I offered Him a hundred exits
in the name of sanity
and He stubbornly refused them all.
I see —
**MORALITY DOES NOT EXIST
UNTIL IT BECOMES A LIABILITY TO YOU.**

Under the ghastly stench of Golgotha,
love was first born in the death throes of a Jew.
Character for humanity was hammered out
by a stained and filthy hill-top mallet.
And every tyrant died
when the thorned head sighed
and burned the scrolls that bore the mark of Caesar.

I know that history will display my head upon a plate.
I saw the changing of the world
but could not prevent my role in it.
But upon my soul, God told me
He wrote no villains in that play.

But should we forget we are divinely bred,
we could well
be reminded
by a highway ribboned with dangling humanity…
be reminded
by the resounding crack of ten thousand hill-top mallets…
be reminded
that each tide moves the banks a bit
closer to the source.

Introduction to "The Assassinations"

American "Camelot" was the fireworks that signaled the end of a boring day and the start of something fantastic. Prior to the arrival of "Golden Jack" Kennedy, there was a father-child relationship between President Dwight D. "Ike" Eisenhower and the American people. It was a James Stewart movie. We were all caricatures. We were boring. Security does that to people.

And when the beautiful crowned prince and princess waltzed into the White House, we were giddy. Leaders are supposed to be the collective personification of the group. We loved ourselves. But a fall is more devastating the higher you fall from. We couldn't get much higher.

In one day, the princess went from regally gowned to frazzled, beaten, with blood-stained stockings. The child in us tried standing again on shaking legs, dizzy from the blow. Then came Viet Nam, the civil rights violence, the assassinations of Martin Luther King and Robert Kennedy. "Blow upon blow of crime and woe and death and war and uncertainty."

Reverend Martin Luther King pulled one way, while the Black Panthers and Elija Muhammed pulled another. The white Right loaded their carbines while the white Left groveled for forgiveness. Our intellectuals, "diplomats", tried to ease national chaos with explanations of cause and effect. The hippies — our folk singers — trying to put it in perspective, "sang of lofty things, but paused with pale uncertainty."

I saw an interview of Patrick Swayze. When asked about his father's death, Patrick explained that no matter how old you are, you are never fully a man until your father dies. When you are finally, painfully, placed on the top of your family tree, all dependency disappears. Growing up and taking the reins is painful.

The Assassinations

The gold-crowned prince we loved,
through multi-purposed deeds did
dance in a veil of blood.
A Dallas ringing cheer of lead,
sent the beautiful knight quite dead.
Let's drop to our wrinkled knees and weep
for the permanent sleep of love.

The writhing back-seat body stung and blown to bits
our hearts were hung in effigy, but not unsung.
But our pitiful songs have not undone
the blood that on the stocking clung;
and it has all only just begun.

Wrapped in sun-reflecting chrome,
gliding by a Dallas home,
the sun fell down on a chunk of lead
and split open young Jack's head
for all to see
the blood drip off his ladie's knee.
Oh, drop to our knees and weep and see
the blood drip off the ladie's knee.
Of course, we say, 'twon't be unsung
but, God, it has all only just be begun.

The same went on with Reverend King,
and the sting that stung young brother Bob;
the "crack" and smoking-barreled curse,
that bile that nursed our festered sores
and increased the blood stains on our floors,
that tore our character, thinly veiled,
and nailed our souls to the chapel door.

Well, our singers sang of lofty things.
Our diplomats as oft would please
our senses with effect and cause,
but they paused with pale uncertainty.

Papa Ike used to hold the hands of us infants snug,
and securely ban all evil from
our sky-blue land of promises.
Then princely Jack, a reflection he,
of our childlike heroic self-imagery,
crooned his golden philosophies.

As all gods must, the gods shook the dust
from our starry-eyed childish dependency
with blow upon blow of crime and woe
and death and war and uncertainty.

Our infant eyes grew steadily clear,
our fear numbed out by suffered pains,
we finally stood up and took the reins
in anger and resolve.

Introduction to Uncle Russ

Dad's brother, Russ   Dad

The cops (including the FBI) had been after my Uncle "Melf" for years. Either nobody knows why or nobody's talking. My dad never told them where Melf was. Neither did Russ, even when they questioned him with such exuberance, he had to be carried up to his Chicago apartment after being discarded on the sidewalk in front. He died a couple of days later. But my family showed 'em that they wouldn't take a thing like that lying down. They all moved to Pittsburgh.

Years later, when my dad's mother died, I wasn't interested in attending the funeral because I never really knew her that well. After I found out that the FBI staked out the service (hoping Melf would show up), I was sorry I never went. I'd never seen a G-Man before.

Uncle Russ

Uncle Russ never made much a fuss,
he was just kinda sorta rambunctious.
The whole Whetsell bunch, when in a crunch
bent the rules without much compunction.

The cops, unamused, and very short-fused,
in Detroit they did rough up my dad.
But that's not so bad, when Russ they did grab
in Chicago and pounded him dead.

Now, none of this mess, you ever would guess,
had to do with those two I detailed.
But was my uncle Melf, a felon himself
so illusive, he never was jailed.

Snappy dressers, but never confessors,
Dad and Russ remained so tight-lipped;
Melf split so fast, the cops were aghast.
that they never knew when he had skipped.

FBI with binocs, surrounded the block
at Granny's memorial service,
hoping that Melf, might show up himself
to pay some respects, although nervous.

Melf vaporized, the cops realized,
and they stopped accosting the clan.
Too late for Russ, since all of this fuss
cost him literally all that he had.

Take My Hand

crossing the street in '51
from habit, my father clutched my hand.
embarrassed, my manly eight-year hand
freed the grasp to search my pocket
for some important thing.
      I knew my search had fooled my dad.

crossing the street in '81
from habit I clutched my son's hand.
embarrassed, his manly eight-year hand
freed the grasp to search his pocket
for some important thing.
      He knew his search had fooled his dad.

I wish I had both chances again.

God Bless Grandpa, Beer, and Mrs. Murphy's Chowder

Magnificently drunk, at seventy six,
he'd plod his way down darkened streets
from the Eagles Lodge,
bellowing a song closely akin to
"Oh, who threw the overalls in Mrs. Murphy's chowder?
And if nobody answers, I'll shout it that much louder!
Oh, it's a dirty Irish trick, and I'll whip the dirty mick who
threw the overalls in Mrs. Murphy's chowder!"

He was soon accompanied by howling dogs
       the length of the town.

And on the couch,
he'd fling pennies and dimes
scattering on the floor
to my pajama-clad sister and me;
which we reluctantly returned
when he grinningly fell asleep...Eagle-flying.

We search for so much
that doesn't exist,
and forget to envy him, who
for fifty years found love and beauty
in a bottle of beer, a bellowing song,
and a woman who welcomed him home
                on Friday nights.

Two Years Since My Father's Death

Two years since my father's death
and I can first suspect there was a man in there
to share some of himself with me.

That quiet figure I grew not to know
the how and why of substance and thought,
was caught never by my mind.

The man who worked and came and sat
and stared in silence, ill-prepared
to share with me his manhood.

So, I stood in reflection of fiction
idols of soldiers and heroes not real,
but there to see.

How does a man love?
I had to guess.
Show fear, compassion, deal with stress?
Talk to a son about quiet things?

The seeds of man's mind I planted alone,
to grow up bent or straight,
no mold to plant boundaries on my acts
never sure of who or what I was
or was to be.

I felt I grew by books or films
or alley tales with friends
who said a man is this….

But reflecting now I see pride
he had in his eyes for
goals I reached

and quietly bragged he said
to friends his boy had
grown up straight and right.

And I know now he hadn't
learned from his fatherless
days how to take me

to the planes of manhood.
He only hoped by fate
and chance I would find it.

I hope I did.

Girl of green fires   Moon song singer

Grandmother and Grandfather Cummings

Married after the turn of the century, my Irish immigrant grandfather (an Irish tenor) died, like many Irish immigrants then, of tuberculosis. "Bright mustang he was," died, coughing, just before his wife "through pain and blood, opened as life pounded at the locks," giving birth to my mother.

In Memory

One remembers the past in snapshots not epochs,
so she thumbed through her 80 years.
Scene upon scene climbed upon age,
not reluctant as a wary child being pushed
by the indifferent hands of hours and days,
but bore the intruding grays of hair
without sighs of despair, just too tired to care.

And today, pale as a winter's sun
and stiff as a spinster's spine
she trudged the bone-creaking stairs
and sat by the window to stare.

There, she — the girl of green fires — once again
ran the park, petticoated in Spring joy
in a world she could buy with a wish
and have glee to spare.

There, the green girl of fires giggled,
red-cheeked and sweet-breathed,
eyes that danced through the day,
to play with princes and marriage,
she was borne by the carriage of her
bright days — down, slowly down.

Slowly, to moon-wooed:
Moon silvered walks, flower scented talks
the lake-sided willow wept with joy.

The moon song singer,
bright mustang he was,
sang away the dust of time.
And brightly united on a bell-ringing Sunday

love leaped loudest on
that loud bell Sabbath.

Days bright as glass,
nights sweet as humming,
then coming through heartbeats,
she — through pain and blood —
opened as life pounded at the locks.

The days whipped windily through
as shoe sizes grew,
but the mustang coughed more than before.
And soon, pale like the winter's sun
— and coughing — the mustang sang back
the dust of time.
The moon singer sang no more.

Now, the home, like Coney Island in winter,
was left behind, blind in the
sad days of dying willows.
She was left, like the home,
with the shoe sizes grown,
which walked their ways.

Now, the girl, not a girl, and the fires
not green, trudged the uncountable stairs;
or walked the park
bent in her print dress and
less, seemingly, than the woman she was,
meeting blank stares…
the blank eyes of pigeons.

Slowly down, the soul sinks back
and the unsupported body sags,
tallow and cheeks and lips,
slips and lays on bone.

Hair, wind-wisped, silk bare,
that staring sapphire sphere
at the window there,
high above the stick-beaten,
chalk-written street of
green girls and princes in sneakers.

There, she calls down the last
feeble-stepping dream—gold bathed.
A soft rustle of wings
fans gently behind her eyes.

So in liquid dreams she lifts off, to the
faint tick-tocking of her willing heart.
Time—killing her softly—the seconds fell
like drops of lead…the soft strum
of a song being sung
by a waiting, missing mustang.

Introduction to What's-His-Name

In the mid-'70s after research on cold-water drownings revealed that victims could be revived if recovered within an hour, I changed our (fire department's) protocols for the dive/rescue team.

I would always have my dive gear with me and respond directly to the scene and go in the water and be joined a few minutes later by the rest of the team. Diving alone—even for a few minutes—is not without risks. If there is anything more idiotic than diving alone under a fish cannery through old, discarded nets, crab pots, cables, and ropes, it's doing it at night without an underwater flashlight.

To What's-His-Name, Aged 24

(who, one stormy November night, fell head-first from the dock)

In the night-freezing drench and black-rolled tide
that called him down through the rain
the twenty-foot plunge to the icy bay
by the dock, by the ship…by himself.

It was so fast and terrifyingly black,
his head-first plunge into the bay,
his fear had seized his voice up tight
and only his heart cried through the night,

"Oh God," his heart cried on the wind,
"I'm dying…if not save me, then
someone go with me as I slip away.
Someone go with me as I die
at the bottom of this black bay."

His slip was seen and the
alarm turned in, still as his heart
beat to the casual fish.
I sped through the night
my siren squawking, "I'm coming."

Amidst a scurry of points and shouts,
the bouts of this fight, I'd fought before,
and I dropped through the floor of the bay
like a rock, and knocked myself flat
in the mud down below.

And there in the black and the cold of the floor
I counted the beats of my heart
and started a prayer for both of our souls
as water rushed in to my ill-donned suit.

My gloveless hands searched through the mud,
my moves became dulled and filled with pain
as I crawled through the wire and ropes and nets
discarded for years from salty decks.
Like brambled fingers snaring their catch
they picked and pulled at my tank and my mask.

I froze from my fear of being tangled up tight
in the cold, in the black and oblivious tide.
Alone was the sound of my iron lung
resound as I clung to the mud…face down.

As I groped, I considered not moving at all.
The call from his soul stopped gripping my ears,
the fear for my soul…I don't know him at all,
I don't owe him one hair of my head.

But machine-like I moved, divorced from my fear
like two different people down in the black;
one to lie still and use up his air,
the other detached and searched on his own.

To inch my way through snags
was to attempt a steady, unswerving march
toward some final truth.
Some Final Truth…
                     —Was it—
         to stare in to the black face of eternity
         and wither back from his cold eyes, or…
                  stare him down?

Send out your black patrol (I dared),
to confront my groping eyes, defy my search,
intimidate my nerve,
I won't shrink back from you!

But don't loom above my head
to attack my back.
Up front! That's how I came to meet you;
                              head first.

With ice in my back and mud on my hands
I search for both of you:
Him, the stranger, and
you, the Final Truth.
But scared as ice I am of you
I won't wither at your stare
I'll be damned if I do.

                      —Or Perhaps it was—
        To sense a man, maybe inches away,
            dying in the unjudging black,
      in the night that doesn't know his name…
      or care. That he should know I search.

                      —Or Perhaps—
          To see clearly we are merely
        the litter life leaves in its passing,
        the leaves trees leave in the fall,
           the world's biggest zero
     in the black bowels of the universe.

                      —Or for me—
That we can be as brave as we want, or scared.
    As resolved as we want, or exempt,
       and it's truly a matter of choice;
to be judged by ourselves in the quiet moments.
      And envy those static creatures
who are never destined to keep appointments
      with their own souls…or choices.

Finally the diving team entered with lights

stabbing the bottom strewn with debris,
and with glimpses of fins and tanks in my sight,
I ascended a pylon swept by the swell,
                       and soon it was done
with divers thrashing the surface
with hands and shouts…and him.

Later, sleepless, I relived his fall
over and over in my mind, until I felt
the terror of his last act as my own,
and wondered why I did.

And to this day, I try to believe
                       …as that Final Truth…

            I did as a way of embracing his soul
             by going with him on his last leap.
          To say to him, "It's sad for you to go alone
           through the black. I fell with you, my friend,
                     to your end."

Genesis on the Book Shelf

Putting aside the debate about man's origin for a minute...Fallen Angel versus Risen Ape...let's look at the following estimates:

Since his appearance on this planet, man has stacked up about eight hundred life-spans. The first seven hundred and forty life-spans were spent in caves or worse. It's only been the last sixty where man had any real shelter. It has been estimated that only in the last forty life-spans has man had any discernable, formal communications. And only the last seven life-spans saw printing. Words.

The spoken word is amazing in its own right: Sounds carried on puffs of breath that not only announce immediate and basic concerns, but transmit abstract concepts from one living person to another. With words, man created the second world; the world of culture. Words painted portraits of the past and graphic visions of the future.

The source of most elation—and dark brooding— is injected into our scrambled psyches via words. The unique greatness and the unique suffering of our species comes from knowledge we are able to pass from one individual to another. "Words" are our Eve's apple; our greatness....our suffering.

Because of words, Man is different from that mute animal whose past vaporizes quickly, and whose entire universe consists of that which lies immediately in front of him. The world of that other animal, contains no abstract anticipation; there is nothing outside his periphery to revere or fear. Nothing exists outside his periphery.

If words were the tools that led to the creation of culture, creation of the abstract, affirmation of the past, the hopes for the future, then the *written* word immortalized the fleeting thought, and institutionalized concepts.

You don't need Genesis to believe in miracles. With the written word, you can sit in your solitude and share a moment or share a dream with someone who has been dead for a thousand years. How's that for a miracle?

www.ingramcontent.com/pod-product-compliance
Lightning Source LLC
Chambersburg PA
CBHW071739040426
42446CB00012B/2399